BOB DYLAN : PIANO SOLO

WISE PUBLICATIONS
part of The Music Sales Group
London / New York / Paris / Sydney / Copenhagen /
Berlin / Madrid / Hong Kong / Tokyo

Blind Willie McTell

Music by Bob Dylan

Blowin' In The Wind

Music by Bob Dylan

Don't Think Twice, It's All Right

Music by Bob Dylan

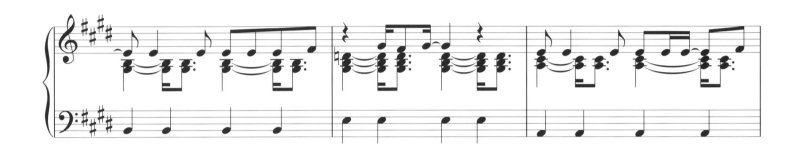

Dignity

Music by Bob Dylan

Forever Young

Music by Bob Dylan

(Instrumental)

Just Like A Woman

Music by Bob Dylan

Coda

Knockin' On Heaven's Door

Music by Bob Dylan

Lay, Lady, Lay

Music by Bob Dylan

To Coda ⊕

D.S. al Coda

⊕ *Coda*

Like A Rolling Stone

Music by Bob Dylan

Make You Feel My Love

Music by Bob Dylan

Not Dark Yet

Music by Bob Dylan

Someday Baby

Music by Bob Dylan

41

Things Have Changed

Music by Bob Dylan

Guitar interlude

The Times They Are A-Changin'

Music by Bob Dylan

When I Paint My Masterpiece

Music by Bob Dylan

Published by
Wise Publications
14-15 Berners Street, London W1T 3LJ, UK.

Exclusive Distributors:
Music Sales Limited
Distribution Centre, Newmarket Road,
Bury St Edmunds, Suffolk IP33 3YB, UK.
Music Sales Pty Limited
20 Resolution Drive, Caringbah, NSW 2229, Australia.

Order No. AM1004641
ISBN: 978-1-78038-524-2
This book © Copyright 2012 Wise Publications,
a division of Music Sales Limited.

Edited by Jenni Norey.
Music arranged by Vasco Hexel.
Music processed by Paul Ewers Music Design.
Cover design by Tim Field.
Cover photograph by Getty Images.
Printed in the EU.

Your Guarantee of Quality

As publishers, we strive to produce every book
to the highest commercial standards.

This book has been carefully designed to minimise awkward
page turns and to make playing from it a real pleasure.

Particular care has been given to specifying
acid-free, neutral-sized paper made from pulps which
have not been elemental chlorine bleached.

This pulp is from farmed sustainable forests and
was produced with special regard for the environment.

Throughout, the printing and binding have been planned
to ensure a sturdy, attractive publication which
should give years of enjoyment.

If your copy fails to meet our high standards,
please inform us and we will gladly replace it.

www.musicsales.com